THE SCALE OF GOOD DEEDS
The Message of the Velāma Sutta

Susan Elbaum Jootla

BUDDHIST PUBLICATION SOCIETY
KANDY   SRI LANKA

Published in 1990

Buddhist Publication Society
P.O. Box 61
Sangharaja Mawatha
Kandy, Sri Lanka

Copyright © 1990
by Susan Elbaum Jootla

ISBN 955-24-0083-x

Typeset at the BPS using an Atari 1040ST
Computer and Signum 2.0 software.
Text set in Antique Roman

Offset in Sri Lanka by
Karunaratne & Sons Ltd.
Colombo 10

THE WHEEL PUBLICATION NO. 372

A NOTE ON SOURCES

The Velāma Sutta is found in the Anguttara Nikāya, Navakanipāta (Collection of Nines), Sutta No. 20 (Pali Text Society edition, Volume IV, pp. 392-96). The rendering given here is based on the translation by E. M. Hare in his rendition of the Anguttara Nikāya, *The Book of Gradual Sayings*, Volume IV, pp. 262-64. I have also consulted Hellmuth Hecker's version in *Anāthapiṇḍika: The Great Benefactor* (BPS Wheel No. 334), pp. 31-32. Quotations from other suttas included in the body of this essay are renderings based on the published translations referred to in each case, most of which are publications of the Pali Text Society. Quotations from the Dhammapada are based on a number of existing English translations. The "Perception of Impermanence," added as an Appendix, is translated by Ven. Bhikkhu Bodhi.

THE VELĀMA SUTTA

A

1. Once, when the Buddha was dwelling near Sāvatthī at Jeta Grove, in Anāthapiṇḍika's park, the householder Anāthapiṇḍika visited him and after greeting him politely sat down at one side.

2. The Exalted One addressed Anāthapiṇḍika, "Are alms given in your house, householder?"

3. "Yes, Lord, alms are given by my family, but it only consists of broken rice and sour gruel."

B

4. "Householder, whether one gives coarse or choice alms, if one gives it without respect, without thought, not by one's own hand, gives only leftovers and without belief in the result of actions, then wherever he is reborn as a result of his having given these alms, his mind will not turn to the enjoyment of fine food and clothing, fine vehicles, or the fine objects of the five senses. His children, wife, servants and labourers will not obey him, and neither listen nor pay attention to him. And why is that so? Because this is the result of actions done without respect.

5. "But whether one gives coarse or choice alms, if one gives it with respect, thoughtfully, by one's own hand, gives things that are not leftovers and with be-

lief in the result of actions, then wherever he is reborn as a result of his having given these alms, his mind will turn to the enjoyment of fine food, clothes and vehicles, and of the finer objects of the five senses. His children, wife, servants and labourers will obey him, listen and pay attention to him. And why is this? Because this is the result of actions done with respect.

C

6. "Long ago, householder, there lived a brahman called Velāma. He gave very valuable gifts such as these: He gave eighty-four thousand golden bowls filled with silver; he gave eighty-four thousand silver bowls filled with gold; he gave eighty-four thousand copper bowls filled with jewels; he gave eighty-four thousand horses with trappings, banners and nets of gold; he gave eighty-four thousand carriages spread with lion skins, tiger skins and leopard skins, with saffron-coloured blankets, with golden trappings, banners and nets; he gave eighty-four thousand milk-giving cows with fine jute ropes and silver milk pails; he gave eighty-four thousand bejeweled maidens; he gave beds with covers of fleece, white blankets, embroidered coverlets, covered with antelope skins, with awnings and with crimson cushions at the ends; he gave eighty-four thousand lengths of cloth of the best flax, silk, wool and cotton. And who could describe all the food both hard and soft kinds, sweets and syrups that he gave? They flowed like rivers.

7. "Perhaps, householder, you think that the brah-

man Velāma who made that very valuable gift was someone else. Do not think that, for it was I who was Velāma the brahman who made that very valuable gift.

D

8. "But when that alms was given, householder, there were no recipients worthy of the gift. Although the brahman Velāma gave such a valuable gift, if he had fed one person of right view, the fruit of the latter deed would have been greater.

9. "Though he gave that very rich gift, or though he fed a hundred people of right view, the fruit of feeding a Once-returner would have been greater.

10. "Though he gave that very valuable gift, or though he fed a hundred Once-returners, the fruit of feeding one Non-returner would have been greater.

11. "... though he fed a hundred Non-returners, the fruit of feeding one Arahat would have been greater.

12. "... though he fed a hundred Arahats, the fruit of feeding one Non-Teaching Buddha would have been greater.

13. "... though he fed a hundred Non-Teaching Buddhas, the fruit of feeding one Perfect One, a Teaching Buddha, would have been greater.

14. "... though he fed one Perfect One, a Teaching Buddha, the fruit of feeding the Order of monks (Sangha) with the Buddha at its head would have been greater.[1]

---

1. § 14 and §16 do not appear in the *Gradual Sayings* text but have been added to complete the sequence. The content of these two paragraphs was dictated by the preceding and succeeding paragraphs.

15. "... though he fed the Order of monks with the Buddha at its head, the fruit of building a monastery for the use of the monks of the Order of the surrounding country would have been greater.

E

16. "... though he built a monastery for the Order, the fruit of sincerely taking refuge in the Buddha, the Dhamma and the Sangha would have been greater.

17. "... though he sincerely took refuge in the Buddha, the Dhamma and the Sangha, the fruit of sincerely undertaking to keep the moral precepts—abstaining from killing, stealing, sexual misconduct, lying and intoxicants causing sloth—would have been greater.

F

18. "... though he sincerely undertook those precepts, the fruit of developing (concentration on radiating universal) lovingkindness (*mettā*) even just to the extent of a whiff of scent, would have been greater.

G

19. "... though he developed lovingkindness to the extent of a whiff of scent, the fruit of cultivating the thought of impermanence—even for the moment of a finger snap—would have been greater."

THE SCALE OF GOOD DEEDS
The Message of the Velāma Sutta

Introduction

In the Velāma Sutta the Buddha provides us with a vivid outline of the relative degrees of merit that can be acquired by performing different kinds of good actions (*kusala kamma*). He does not discuss the specific results produced by meritorious deeds, but only their relative gradation. While his outline is lightly sketched, its implications are extensive and profound.

Good actions are bodily deeds, spoken words, or thoughts accompanied by wholesome volition (*kusala cetanā*). Wholesome volition may be rooted in the mental factors of non-greed (or detachment), non-hatred (or goodwill), or non-delusion (wisdom). Sections A, B, C and D of the Velāma Sutta deal with bodily good deeds: various kinds of charity, generosity or giving, all included in the Pali word *dāna*. Section E deals with verbal good deeds: taking the Triple Refuge and undertaking the Five Precepts, which are usually formally done aloud, either alone or by repeating them after a monk or teacher. Sections F and G concern purely mental good deeds, as both deal with aspects of meditation. Mental actions can be very powerful, and the Buddha points out that proper development of concentration (*samādhi*) and wisdom (*paññā*) generate the most potent good results (*vipāka*) of all the many kinds of wholesome kamma.

Good kammas bring good future results to the doer in accordance with the natural moral law of cause and effect. Likewise, bad actions yield bad future results in the form of different kinds of suffering. The degree and kind of beneficial result (*vipāka*) or fruit (*phala*) varies widely with the kind and quality of the good kamma or merit (*puñña*) that has been performed. In the Velāma Sutta the Buddha devotes the greater part of his exposition to giving; Sections A, B, C and D all discuss this most basic kind of wholesome deed. Morality (*sīla*) is dealt with in Section E, concentration (*samādhi*) in Section F, and wisdom or insight (*paññā, vipassanā*) in Section G. These are the four major categories that include all kinds of wholesome kamma. Together they make up the Noble Eightfold Path, which is the Buddha's prescription for putting an end to suffering.[2]

Giving

In the Velāma Sutta the Buddha is speaking to his leading lay disciple, the great donor and rich merchant of Sāvatthī who was known as Anāthapiṇḍika. Anāthapiṇḍika was already renowned as a generous giver of charity to the Buddha and his monks (*bhikkhus*) and also to the poor people of the area.

---

2. The eight factors of the noble path are generally divided into a wisdom section (right view and right thought); a morality section (right speech, right action and right livelihood—giving might be loosely included in right action and going for refuge in right speech); and a concentration section (right effort, right mindfulness and right concentration).

Our sutta begins (Section A) with the Buddha asking the layman whether *dāna*, specifically alms food, is given by his household. Anāthapiṇḍika replies that such charity is given but it consists of only very coarse kinds of food. The commentary explains that he is here referring to the alms his family gives to the needy who come to their door, not to the much finer gifts they customarily donate to the Sangha, the Order of Buddhist monks. Another possible explanation for the poor quality of the alms that Anāthapiṇḍika mentions is that this conversation took place at a time when his vast assets had been greatly diminished through a series of misfortunes that drained him of almost all his wealth. At the same time, because of his natural compassion, he was reluctant to press his debtors to repay their debts, and many took advantage of his kindness. Even during this period of stringency for his household, this great benefactor made it a point to give food to the monks daily, but he could only afford plain, simple fare, not the rich curries and sweets he offered to them during more prosperous times.[3]

If this second explanation for the poor almsfood given by Anāthapiṇḍika's family is accepted, then Section B of the discourse may be understood as the Buddha's way of reassuring him that even though at the moment he could not give sumptuous food, he would still continue to earn much merit from his offerings so long as he gave them with the proper mental attitude.

---
3. See *Anāthapiṇḍika*, p. 9, referring to Jātaka No. 284.

The proper approach to giving and the kammic results it brings form the substance of Section B of the Velāma Sutta. The Buddha explains what kind of giving will bring full benefit according to the kammic law, and what kind will not. In all its varieties, *dāna* is always a meritorious action that leads to pleasant results. Defined very broadly in the Buddhist texts, *dāna* includes not only the giving of material gifts, but also the giving of one's time and energy in voluntary service and the teaching of the Dhamma. It even includes giving other beings freedom from fear by being non-violent oneself.

Whether or not the gift itself is valuable in monetary terms is irrelevant to the Buddha's analysis, as shown by the phrase "whether one gives coarse or choice alms" at the beginning of both paragraphs in Section B. In other sermons the Buddha says that if the value of a gift is proportionate to the donor's financial situation, that is both appropriate and sufficient. A small gift from a poor person can create as much good kamma as a large gift from a wealthy one. A meager gift from a prince would bring a poor acquisition of good kamma, while if a poor man shared the last cup of rice in his house with someone else this could be extremely beneficial.

In the Velāma Sutta the Buddha deals first with gifts which will not bring as much merit as they would if offered properly (§ 4). A gift of any quality, fancy or plain, will give only limited future benefits if it is given casually, without respect; thoughtlessly, in an impolite way; by having another person hand it over; if it is left over from one's own meal; or if it is given without considering and understanding the law of kamma and its fruits, "belief in the result of actions" in the words of the sutta. This last is the most important of these five factors.

Even if the result of such a gift puts the donor in a position where—in a subsequent life—he receives fine food, clothes and vehicles, and he lives in comfortable circumstances and good health, the Buddha states that he may not be able to enjoy these things. In addition, at this time his children and the people who work for him will not listen to him or pay attention to what he says. The Buddha declares that this happens because such is the natural kammic result of actions performed without respect. In other words, a person who gives in such a haphazard way will not be able to enjoy or appreciate the pleasant results which the act of generosity is bound to bring him.

An example of this is a certain miser discussed in a series of conversations between King Pasenadi of Kosala and the Buddha.[4] The king describes a very wealthy man in Sāvatthī who had recently died without making arrangements for anyone to inherit his property. Under these circumstances Kosalan law provided that the king was entitled to confiscate the entire fortune; he had just done so when he came to see the Buddha. King Pasenadi mentioned all this to the Buddha because the dead man had been known to be very miserly, even towards himself. He lived as though he were indigent, wearing the roughest kind

---

4. In the Kosala Saṁyutta. *Kindred Sayings*, I, pp. 115-17.

of clothes, eating stale food, and using the cheapest kind of carriage.

In reply the Buddha told King Pasenadi that once, in the distant past, this man had given food to a Non-Teaching Buddha but had regretted his deed immediately afterwards, thinking, "It would have been better if my slaves and workers had eaten it." The offering of this gift to such a wise being had led to his rebirth several times in the celestial planes, and subsequently as an eminently rich man in Sāvatthi. However, the unwholesome kamma generated by his subsequent regret resulted in his miserly temperament and "inclined his heart to denying himself excellent food, clothes, carriages and enjoyment of sense pleasures."

In §5 of the Velāma Sutta the Buddha tells Anāthapiṇḍika that if one gives fresh food, considerately, with one's own hands, and after thinking about the deed and with belief in kamma and its fruit, then wherever that almsgiving brings its fruit in future births, the giver's mind will be able to appreciate the sense pleasures available to him, and his children, wife and workers will be obedient and cooperative. This is the opposite of the result of carelessly performed charity. Both are good deeds, but the accompanying states of mind are poles apart, and this influences the result.

It is interesting to note that the Buddha teaches that for ordinary householders, legitimately earned pleasures of the senses—attractive sights, sounds, smells, tastes, or tangibles—need not be avoided when they do not entail breaking the Five Precepts.

Such pleasurable feelings are simply facts of life, the result of our previous good deeds. If they have been earned they might as well be enjoyed; there is no "sin" involved as long as the Five Precepts are scrupulously kept.[5] Being miserly creates even worse kamma than spending reasonably on oneself and one's dependents; sharing one's earned wealth, of course, is good kamma.

The Gifts of Velāma

In Section C the Buddha provides a story from the past to illustrate the practice of generosity. He describes the incredibly lavish gifts he bestowed in one of his previous existences when, as a Bodhisatta developing the perfection of giving (*dāna pāramī*), he was reborn as the brahman Velāma. Velāma's gifts included gold and silver, valuable domestic animals, fancy chariots and luxurious beds. Velāma also gave away food and drink in vast quantities.

The Buddha points out to Anāthapiṇḍika in Section D that even though Velāma's generosity was vast and his gifts were given properly (in accordance with the guidelines in Section B), the results were not as complete as they might have been under different circumstances. In Velāma's time there were no beings available who were, in the most eminent sense, truly worthy to receive his gifts. The proper recipient

---

5. Unwholesome—*akusala*—kamma associated with desire, *taṇhā* or *lobha*, may be generated however. But for the ordinary householder this kind of relatively weak bad kamma is unavoidable a great deal of the time.

would have been an Ariya, a Noble One—one who had attained to any of the four stages of holiness by purifying his mind of defilements. The Buddha continues to develop, throughout the rest of this section, this same theme: that the purity of the recipient is an essential factor that influences the amount of merit earned by an act of generosity.

A series of verses in the Dhammapada make a similar point (vv. 106-108). In these stanzas, it is said that simply paying sincere respect to Ariyas is far more meritorious than making sacrifices, tending ritual fires, or giving gifts to non-Ariyas. Respectfully giving a gift to an Ariya must be even more profitable than bowing to one, although such *dāna* does not figure in these lines.

> Whatever gifts and oblations one seeking merit might offer in this world for a whole year, all that is not worth one fourth of the merit gained by revering the Upright Ones (Ariyas), which is truly excellent.
>
> (Dhp. 108)

While the Buddha was alive and for as long as his teachings are practised, individuals of great purity arise in the world and gifts to them bring the greatest merit that can be earned through generosity. Although it may be hard to find Ariyas today, people who keep the moral precepts (*sīla*), practise concentration (*samādhi*), and cultivate wisdom (*paññā*) are certainly available. Such individuals, whether monks or laypeople, share to some extent in the characteristics of Ariyas. For this reason, gifts to them should bear greater fruit than gifts to ordinary folk who make no effort to improve themselves. Wandering ascetics as well as priests may or may not live morally and they may or may not strive to develop concentration and wisdom. Hence it is uncertain whether such recipients will endow a gift with the maximum of profit for the donor.

From Section D through the rest of the sutta the Buddha describes a scale or hierarchy of meritorious deeds. This scale of merit begins with Velāma's gifts as the broad base, and then ascends by degrees culminating in the wisdom that knows the truth of impermanence (*anicca*).

Above the greatest gift given to non-Ariyas comes feeding different categories of Ariyas. Giving nourishment to beings with such pure minds is a very valuable source of merit. In § 8 the Buddha says that the fruit of feeding a single person of right view would be greater than the fruit of Velāma's vast generosity given to ordinary worldlings. A person of right view is the first kind of Ariya, a Stream-enterer (*sotāpanna*), one assured of liberation in a maximum of seven lifetimes. A Stream-enterer keeps the Five Precepts perfectly; possesses full faith in the Buddha, Dhamma and Sangha; has thoroughly understood that everything comes about as a result of causes and conditions; and has thereby eliminated three defilements from his mental continuum.

These three defilements are: the incorrect view that affirms a lasting self or soul; all doubt about the way to liberation; and the belief that rites and rituals can lead to liberation. It is eliminating belief in a self that gives the Stream-enterer the title "one of right view."

The Buddha goes through the remaining three higher kinds of Ariya in order: the Once-returner (*sakadāgāmī*), who has greatly attenuated sense desire and ill will; the Non-returner (*anāgāmī*), who has totally uprooted these two defilements; and the fully liberated Arahat, who has eradicated all traces of greed, hatred and ignorance and all other mental impurities. The Buddha states that feeding one of each higher stage brings greater rewards than feeding a hundred on the stage just below.

The greatest recipients, named next, are Buddhas, beings who attain liberation unaided by discovering the ultimate truths about existence for themselves without the guidance of a teacher. There are two kinds of Buddhas, Non-Teaching Buddhas (*paccekabuddha*) and universal Buddhas who instruct other beings (*sammā-sambuddha*), like Gotama Buddha. Any number of Pacceka-buddhas can exist at one time in the world, but they only arise during periods when there is no Sammā-sambuddha living and when the teachings of one are not available, i.e. when no Buddha Sāsana is extant. However, there can only be one Sammā-sambuddha at a time. The Buddha declares that because of his superior stature, feeding a Sammā-sambuddha brings greater results than feeding a hundred Pacceka-buddhas. However, the act of *dāna* that is the most beneficial of all is not a gift of food but constructing a monastery for the use of the Sangha with the Buddha at its head.

During his life Anāthapiṇḍika performed virtually

all the acts of generosity named in the sutta. Shortly after his first encounter with the Buddha he purchased a park known as Jeta Grove (Jetavana) and had a large monastery built there. He then donated the property to the Buddha and the community of monks. Anāthapiṇḍika always gave almsfood, robes and medicine to the monks who came to stay at Jetavana; among those bhikkhus were the greatest Arahat disciples of the Buddha as well as numerous other Noble Ones.

Morality—The Refuges & Precepts

The hierarchy of merit generated by different forms of good kamma continues beyond generosity and culminates in the final three sections of the Velāma Sutta, E, F and G. Even greater than the fruit of Velāma's gifts, or of feeding any kind and number of Noble Ones, or of building a monastery for the Order, is the merit earned from sincerely going for refuge to the Triple Gem, the first step taken by anyone who considers himself a Buddhist (Section E).

The value of going for refuge to the Awakened One, to the Truth embodied in his Teaching, and to the community of those who are following his Teaching—the Buddha, the Dhamma and the Sangha—can be vast if it is accompanied by full comprehension: "He who has gone for refuge to the Buddha, his Teaching and his Order penetrates with wisdom the Four Noble Truths—suffering, the cause of suffering, the cessation of suffering, and the Noble Eightfold Path leading to the cessation of suffering" (Dhp.

190-91). This means that going for refuge with understanding can result in penetration of the Four Noble Truths. If one considers the Buddha and Dhamma as one's protection, one will naturally try to follow those teachings and practise the way to the utter cessation of suffering, which he devoted his life to explaining. One will try to comprehend the first noble truth and to eliminate the second truth by developing the fourth truth, the path, until the third noble truth has been realized.

By taking refuge one enters the way to liberation shown by the Buddha. Giving can be practised even during the vast periods of cosmic history when no Buddha Sāsana is available, as Velāma's story illustrates. Charity is, after all, central to virtually every religion, to every code of good conduct; it is not exclusively Buddhist. But obviously, one can only take the Triple Refuge while the Buddha-Dhamma is available; at other times the Refuges would be inaccessible.

The Velāma Sutta's elisions in § 17 leave some doubt about the exact relationship between going for refuge and keeping the precepts (*sīla*) in the hierarchy of meritorious deeds. Although I have remained close to Hare's translation in my rendering, Hecker says that taking the Triple Refuge "would be perfected if one observed the Five Precepts."[6] The Venerable Ñāṇamoli's translation combines the two in a slightly different way: "Yet it is still more fruitful to go with a confident heart for refuge to the Buddha, Dhamma

---

6. *Anāthapiṇḍika*, p. 32.

and Sangha and undertake the Five Precepts of virtue."[7] The Refuges and the Precepts are closely connected steps of basic Buddhist practice, so regardless of the rendering, we can be confident that the undertaking of the Five Precepts here is additional to rather than a replacement for the going for refuge.

The Five Precepts, the minimum moral requirement for a Buddhist layman, consist of abstaining from doing things that would hurt others, from deeds that lead to one's own rebirth in the lower realms where there is unremitting and intense suffering. To undertake the Five Precepts, one declares: "I will refrain from killing, stealing, sexual misconduct, lying and the use of intoxicants," and then observes them to the best of one's ability. Taking the Refuges when one's morality is pure combines two valuable actions which can produce abundant long-term fruits.

Concentration—Lovingkindness

But greater still than mere morality is the merit earned from proper meditation, and it is meditation or "mental development" (*bhāvanā*) that comprises the highest two rungs in the Buddha's ladder of meritorious actions. These rungs are referred to in the concluding sections, F and G, of the Velāma Sutta. Concentration obtained by extending universal lovingkindness (*mettābhāvanā*), even briefly, is of greater benefit than keeping the precepts; but without the

---

7. Bhikkhu Ñāṇamoli, "Anicca according to Theravada," in *Impermanence: Collected Essays* (BPS Wheel No. 186/187), p. 71.

base of perfect morality such meditation would be impossible. The sutta indicates the short span of *mettā* needed to give results greater than those accruing from keeping the precepts with the phrase "a whiff of scent." In the commentary the analogy used is: for only as long as it takes someone milking a cow to give one pull on her teat. Both images suggest a brief moment. So valuable is the practice of *mettā* that even this slight development of it, done properly, brings the practitioner a vast amount of merit.

In a discourse in the *Kindred Sayings* the Buddha points out, in a similar manner, that such a brief radiation of *mettā* is kammically far more rewarding than giving a large gift:

> If anyone, brethren, were to give a morning gift of a hundred coins, and the same at noon and the same in the evening, or if anyone were to practise in the morning, at noon or in the evening a heart of love (*mettā*), even if it were as slight as one pull at a cow's udder, this practice would be by far the more fruitful of the two.
> (*Kindred Sayings*, II, pp. 176–77)

Concentration practised to the highest level issues in the jhānas, the meditative absorptions. Jhāna is one-pointed, alert absorption in the object. All sensory input is cut off and the mind, "secluded from sense pleasures, secluded from unwholesome states," dwells exclusively fixed upon its chosen object, free from extraneous thoughts. But by itself jhāna can lead only to mundane benefits, such as peace and bliss in the present life and an exalted rebirth in the lofty planes of the Brahma-world, where life endures for extremely long periods of time. It does not necessarily lead to liberation.

Concentration on *mettā* is a highly effective means to attain jhāna, and is also one of the most potent sources of wholesome kamma. In fact, among all purely mundane types of merit, the Buddha praises the meditation on *mettā* as supreme, in a passage which also underscores its inherent limitations:

> Bhikkhus, whatever kinds of merit there are, undertaken with a view to rebirth, all of them are not worth one sixteenth part of the heart's release of lovingkindness; in shining and beaming and radiance the heart's release of lovingkindness far excels them.[8]

"Heart's release of lovingkindness" refers to the temporary suppression of mental defilements by concentration on *mettā*. "With a view to rebirth" means aiming at a happy or pleasant rebirth as a result of the merit earned by good kamma.

But all rebirth keeps the round of suffering (*dukkha*) rolling on, and the Buddha's unique teaching aims at permanently eliminating all suffering. Repeated existence is ultimately and inevitably suffering. All beings who are born must grow old, suffer from disease, and eventually die. Even Brahmās, who

---

8. *Itivuttaka*, No. 27, *As It Was Said*, p. 13; see too *The Practice of Lovingkindness (Mettā)*, Ñāṇamoli Thera (Wheel No. 7), p. 16.

enjoy exceedingly long and blissful lives as the fruits of cultivating the jhānas, will die and be reborn in other planes of existence, over and over again. *Saṁsāra*, for all beings, is an ever-repeated process of birth and death, involving suffering, pain, insecurity and impermanence. Only wisdom can enable us to break out of this vicious cycle. Concentration alone, for all its ability to bring pleasant results, cannot cut the sequence of birth, death and rebirth. Concentration that does not lead to insight in the long run only perpetuates suffering by providing yet more fuel for rebirth. For this reason, the Buddha tells Anāthapiṇḍika (in Section G of the sutta) that the thought of impermanence, which is one aspect of wisdom, creates the greatest good kamma of all meritorious actions.

Wisdom—Insight into Impermanence

If Velāma had been able to meditate directly on impermanence (*anicca*) in his mind or body just for the span of a finger-snap, it would have brought him greater fruit than all the other good deeds mentioned in all the preceding paragraphs of the sutta. But such wisdom was lost to the world in Velāma's time, as he lived during the empty aeons between the arising of two Buddhas. Therefore he had no access to such understanding.

Why is knowing impermanence for oneself of such consummate value? In other discourses that deal specifically with cultivating insight into impermanence the Buddha provides several answers.

First, contemplating impermanence brings the meditator happiness greater than all worldly pleasure because he realizes that with such contemplation he is now moving towards the cessation of all suffering:

> Whenever with insight he sees the rise and fall of the aggregates, he experiences joy and happiness. To the discerning one this reflects the Deathless (Nibbāna).
>
> (Dhp. 374)

Seeing "the rise and fall of the aggregates" is meditating on the transient (*anicca*) nature of all the components of the personality. Such insight brings detachment from these insubstantial phenomena. Great joy arises in the mind thus freed of desire and aversion. The meditator realizes that when his mind becomes utterly and permanently liberated from these defilements, Nibbāna will be attained.

The second reason for the great value of knowing impermanence is that this insight enables one to develop the Noble Eightfold Path all the way to its ultimate goal—the cessation of suffering. In one discourse in the *Gradual Sayings* the Buddha describes six benefits of developing insight into impermanence which convince a monk or meditator that he should cultivate this practice to perfection:

> When a monk sees six rewards it should be enough for him to establish without reserve the thought of impermanence in all phenomena. What six?
>
> (1) All phenomena will seem to me insubstantial;

(2) my mind will find no relish in all the world;
(3) my mind will emerge from all the world;
(4) my mind will incline towards Nibbāna, extinction;
(5) my fetters will come to be abandoned; and
(6) I shall be endowed with the supreme state of a recluse.[9]

The first reward leads the meditator to understand the other two characteristics common to all phenomena: *dukkha* or unsatisfactoriness, and *anattā* or essencelessness. Phenomena are all compounded and conditioned formations (*sankhāra*) and the meditator dwelling on impermanence sees that everything within and around him is conditioned by other things all of which are unstable. As he sees that all the causes are impermanent, he comes to realize that the resulting phenomena must likewise be transient and so without lasting substance, "insubstantial." That which is impermanent and without substance cannot be said to have a lasting essence, so it is not self, *anattā*. That which is unstable cannot be a source of lasting happiness, so it is unsatisfactory, *dukkha*.

The second reward is the undermining of *taṇhā*, craving, which by relishing and delighting in mundane things of all sorts keeps the mind bound to the round of rebirth in a perpetual search for pleasure and self-perpetuation. Where there is no craving for sense objects, one fears the risk of involvement with them and so develops detachment and disgust towards

---

9. *Gradual Saying*, III, p. 308; see Wheel No. 186/187, p. 71

sensual delights. This leads to the third reward: when the mind seeks an alternative to the misery of impermanent existence it tends to disengage itself from everything mundane and so to break away from all the world. The fourth reward of knowing impermanence is the converse of the third: the mind with no interest in worldly matters turns towards the supramundane, the unconditioned, Nibbāna.

The fifth reward is the destruction of the fetters which bind beings to the round of rebirth, saṁsāra. The ten fetters (saṁyojana) are: personality belief, skeptical doubt, clinging to rites and rituals, craving for sense pleasures, ill-will, craving for existence in the fine material planes, craving for existence in the immaterial planes, conceit, restlessness and ignorance. Knowledge of impermanence can in time eliminate all these mental defilements through the four stages of enlightenment.

The sixth reward refers to Arahatship, the culmination of the other five. This is the state of perfect purity in which no defiling tendencies remain and all possibility of future rebirth has been cut off.

In this way, fully understanding how everything that makes up oneself and the external world is utterly unstable can lift the mind to a level of complete and permanent purity. This is the prime reason why, in the final paragraph of the Velāma Sutta, the Buddha declares that the fruit of even a moment's insight into impermanence brings the greatest of all kammic results. Every moment spent knowing impermanence through insight brings one closer to the goal of total liberation.

In a discourse in the *Kindred Sayings* the Buddha explains how consistently and deeply knowing *anicca* in insight meditation (*vipassanā*) can lead all the way to Arahatship.

> Perceiving impermanence, bhikkhus, developed and frequently practised, removes all sensual desire, removes all desire for material existence, removes all desire for becoming, removes all ignorance, and tears out all conceit of "I am."
> (*Kindred Sayings*, III, p. 132)

Developing the understanding of *anicca* gradually eliminates every trace of craving, desire, aversion, and attachment; for as the meditator comes to realize the transience of all aspects of life, he finds sense objects and all prospects of rebirth profoundly unsatisfactory, *dukkha*. One who has eliminated the craving for sense pleasures is a Non-returner (*anāgāmi*), who will never be reborn in the sensuous realms of existence, among humans or *devas*, since his mind no longer has the slightest interest in the sense objects which characterize these realms. Non-returners generally take birth in the Pure Abodes, the highest planes of the fine-material world, which are reserved for such great beings. So attaining the stage of Non-returner and rebirth in the Pure Abodes are among the blessings that come from profound insight into impermanence.

Non-returners attain Arahatship by developing further the perception of impermanence in order to remove attraction towards life even in the exalted planes of existence. This corresponds to the other two kinds of desire mentioned in the quotation—desire for material existence and desire for becoming. Simultaneously, every trace of ignorance is eradicated and every remnant of the deluding conceit "I am" is ripped out of the mind. This is the highest good, the ultimate goal of the Buddha's teaching, Arahatship, the living experience of Nibbāna. This total cessation of suffering can come about through perfect understanding of *anicca*.

How can the insight into impermanence eliminate conceit (*māna*)? When the transience of everything we habitually cling to as "I" and "me" is clearly and repeatedly understood, the actual essencelessness (*anattā*) of the supposed "self" becomes perfectly apparent. Thus, fully developed insight into impermanence brings the great benefit of insight into essencelessness, and full comprehension of essencelessness brings liberation:

> For a monk, Meghiya, who thinks on impermanence, the thought of not-self (*anattā*) endures; thinking on there being no self, he wins to the state wherein the conceit "I am" has been uprooted, to the cool (Nibbāna), even in this life.
>
> (*Gradual Sayings*, IV, p. 237)

Without completely and continually understanding that there is no essence, core or self anywhere for anyone, liberation from the round of existence is impossible. As the Buddha told Meghiya, an effective way to come to comprehend the truth of not-self is through knowing the truth of impermanence. This is because it is easier to recognize impermanence on an intellectual level and also easier to experience it for oneself in insight meditation.

These are the reasons the wisdom of knowing impermanence is so potent that cultivating it even for a short moment gives the greatest results among all the types of meritorious action. All the other good kammas mentioned by the Buddha in the Velāma Sutta may or may not be associated with liberating wisdom. But knowing impermanence is itself an aspect of wisdom or insight, and such wisdom, by its very nature, gradually eliminates ignorance. True insight must tend towards detachment and ultimately towards Nibbāna, the absolute peace that comes with the ending of all the causes of suffering.

Now that we have seen why insight into *anicca* is of such profound value, it will become clear that its results must transcend those of all other kinds of good kammas. Good actions not rooted in wisdom will bear fruit in pleasant existences accompanied by sense pleasures in the human and celestial planes, as the Buddha mentioned in Section B of the Velāma Sutta. Generosity in all its forms, taking the Triple Refuge, keeping the Five Precepts, and even developing the lower levels of concentration—these may be done without wisdom. If they are performed in such a way they serve to perpetuate the round of rebirth. If they are accompanied by wisdom consciously aimed at Nibbāna, they will tend towards liberation from the round. The jhānas, meditative absorptions, are always associated with a degree of wisdom, but this wisdom does not constitute the kind of insight that leads out of *samsāra*. Only if the meditator, upon emerging from a jhāna, examines that state of mind and sees it as impermanent, unsatisfactory, and essenceless (*anicca*, *dukkha*, *anattā*), will the jhāna tend towards release from all suffering.

To illustrate: if gifts are given with the sole aim of obtaining pleasure in the celestial planes, that aim may come to fulfillment, but its fulfillment merely keeps the donor revolving in *saṁsāra*. Though he may live pleasantly, in relative comfort, as long as his merit bears fruit, when that fruit has been exhausted, as it must sooner or later, he is bound to fall again into the lower realms; he may even be reborn into the hells of the most intense suffering. This is because everyone has a backlog of unwholesome kamma awaiting an opportunity to bear fruit. So many of the volitional actions of body, speech and thought that we perform now are also unwholesome (*akusala*), as they are associated with some degree of greed, hatred or delusion, and unwholesome kamma will cause painful rebirths.

By contrast, cultivating insight into impermanence, suffering, and essencelessness leads one out of the round of rebirth towards liberation from all suffering. Deep understanding of the ultimate impermanence of all existence creates a kind of kamma whose tendency is to eliminate all past kamma, good and bad, and so makes liberation possible, as we have already seen. Such insight works towards the state where no more kamma will be created at all.

And what Puṇṇa ... is the kamma that conduces to the destruction of kamma? Where, Puṇṇa,

> there is the volition to get rid of unwholesome kamma, wholesome kamma and mixed kamma ... this Puṇṇa is called ... the kamma that conduces to the destruction of kamma.
>
> (*Middle Length Sayings*, II, p. 58)

The Arahat makes no new kamma; his mind is free of the ignorance that underlies the unenlightened mind, so his thoughts and intentions are merely functional and do not bring any kammic results.

Giving, taking the Triple Refuge, keeping the Five Precepts, and practising concentration all have essential roles to play in maturing one's spiritual faculties so that one can cultivate the understanding of the true nature of existence—the marks of impermanence, suffering, and non-self. The earlier stages cannot be dispensed with; the Buddha taught that morality is to be constantly observed and concentration to be continually strengthened. Otherwise any apparent "insight" that arises will not be pure and deep enough to bring about the cessation of craving. Only when insight has a solid base of merit will it be powerful enough to penetrate the thick murk of ignorance that keeps us thinking "I am permanent" or "I am real."

Conclusion

As a devoted lay Buddhist, Anāthapiṇḍika was well known for his generosity; the name by which he is known to us is actually an epithet meaning "one who gives alms to the unprotected," to the poor. He gave open-handedly to all beings and especially to the Buddha and his monks. Anāthapiṇḍika had firm confidence in the enlightenment of the Buddha, in the truth of the Dhamma he taught, and in the purity of the Sangha. Thus he sincerely took refuge in the Triple Gem. He also kept the Five Precepts at all times, so his morality was excellent.

In the Velāma Sutta the Buddha may be indirectly telling Anāthapiṇḍika that he should not lose sight of the ultimate goal through his devotion to the endless possibilities of mundane good deeds, since these can only bring mundane, temporary results. He is reminding the lay follower that the meditation on lovingkindness for cultivating concentration, and the meditation on impermanence for cultivating insight, are by far the greatest sources of profound merit. By showing Anāthapiṇḍika this ladder of good deeds, the Teacher may have been urging the layman at this stage of his life to devote more effort to mental purification.

Giving gifts, taking the Refuges, and keeping the Precepts are essential to build the foundation of good kamma. But the way out of the misery of the round of repeated births is to develop a mind sufficiently concentrated to penetrate the ultimate truth. It is by fully comprehending the impermanent, unsatisfactory, and essenceless nature of all things in all the planes of conditioned existence that the final goal, the Deathless, is to be won.

Better a single day of life perceiving how things rise and fall than to live a century without ever perceiving their rise and fall.

(Dhp. 113)

APPENDIX

PERCEPTION OF IMPERMANENCE
(Saṁyutta Nikāya, 22:102)

At Sāvatthī the Blessed One said:

"Bhikkhus, when the perception of impermanence is developed and cultivated, it eliminates all sensual lust, it eliminates all attachment to material form, it eliminates all ignorance, it uproots all conceit 'I am.'

"Just as, bhikkhus, in the autumn a ploughman ploughing with a great ploughshare cuts through all the network of roots as he ploughs, so too, when the perception of impermanence is developed and cultivated, it eliminates all sensual lust ... it uproots all conceit 'I am.'

"Just as a cutter of reeds would cut down a reed, grab it by its top, and shake it down and shake it out and thump it about, so too, when the perception of impermanence is developed and cultivated, it eliminates all sensual lust ... it uproots all conceit 'I am.'

"Just as, when the stalk of a bunch of mangoes has been cut, all the mangoes attached to the stalk follow along with it, so too, when the perception of impermanence is developed and cultivated, it eliminates all sensual lust ... it uproots all conceit 'I am.'

"Just as all the rafters of a peaked house lead to the roof peak, slope towards the roof peak and converge upon the roof peak, and the roof peak is declared to be their chief, so too, when the perception of impermanence is developed and cultivated, it eliminates all sensual lust ... it uproots all conceit 'I am.'

"Just as, of all fragrant roots, black fragrant *anusārī* is declared to be their chief, so too, when the perception of impermanence is developed and cultivated, it eliminates all sensual lust ... it uproots all conceit 'I am.'

"Just as, of all fragrant heartwoods, red sandalwood is declared to be their chief, so too, when the perception of impermanence is developed and cultivated, it eliminates all sensual lust ... it uproots all conceit 'I am.'

"Just as, of all fragrant flowers, the jasmine is declared to be their chief, so too, when the perception of impermanence is developed and cultivated, it eliminates all sensual lust ... it uproots all conceit 'I am.'

"Just as all petty princes are the vassals of a Wheel-turning Monarch and the Wheel-turning Monarch is declared to be their chief, so too, when the perception of impermanence is developed and cultivated, it eliminates all sensual lust ... it uproots all conceit 'I am.'

"Just as the radiance of all the stars does not amount to a sixteenth part of the radiance of the moon, and the radiance of the moon is declared to be their chief, so too, when the perception of impermanence is developed and cultivated, it eliminates all sensual lust ... it uproots all conceit 'I am.'

"Just as, in the autumn, when the sky is clear and cloudless, the sun rises above the earth dispelling all darkness from space as it shines and beams and radiates, so too, when the perception of impermanence is developed and cultivated, it eliminates all sensual lust, it eliminates all attachment to material form, it eliminates all attachment to being, it eliminates all ignorance, it uproots all conceit 'I am.'

"And how, bhikkhus, is the perception of impermanence developed and cultivated so that it eliminates all sensual lust ... and uproots all conceit 'I am'?

" 'Such is material form, such its origin, such its passing away; such is feeling, such its origin, such its passing away; such is perception, such its origin, such its passing away; such are mental formations, such their origin, such their passing away; such is consciousness, such its origin, such its passing away' — that is how the perception of impermanence is developed and cultivated so that it eliminates all sensual lust, eliminates all attachment to material form, eliminates all attachment to being, eliminates all ignorance, and uproots all conceit 'I am.' "

ABOUT THE AUTHOR

Susan Elbaum Jootla is an American Buddhist living in northern India and a long-term practitioner of vipassana meditation in the tradition of Sayagyi U Ba Khin. Her previous BPS publications are:

"Right Livelihood" in *The Buddhist Layman* (Wh 294/295)

Investigation for Insight (Wh 301/302)

Inspiration from Enlightened Nuns (Wh 349/350)

"The Practice of Giving" in *Dāna: The Practice of Giving* (Wh 367/369)

On Pilgrimage (BL 118)

Available from BPS

LAST DAYS OF THE BUDDHA
The Mahā Parinibbāna Sutta

The Mahā Parinibbāna Sutta is the Pali Canon's account of the final events in the life of the Buddha. Beginning on Vultures' Peak near the royal capital of Rajagaha, the narrative follows him on his last stirring journey to the small jungle township where he was to attain his final passing away.

During his long ministry the Buddha had taught all that was necessary to reach the goal. In this last phase of his life his primary concern was to impress on his disciples the need to put those same teachings into practice. By his inspiring sermons and serene composure in meeting his end, the Buddha offers the highest possible testimony to his teaching.

This new BPS edition has been freshly revised to improve readability and includes helpful explanatory notes.

120 pages *ISBN 955-24-0006-6*
Softback *Price as in latest catalog*

Available from BPS

BUDDHIST DICTIONARY
Manual of Buddhist Terms and Doctrines

Nyanatiloka Thera

Since its first publication in 1952, *Buddhist Dictionary* has been a trusted companion and helper in the study of Buddhist literature. The author, the well-known German scholar-monk Nyanatiloka Thera (1879-1957), was qualified as few others have ever been to serve as a reliable guide through the field of Buddhist terminology and doctrine. This book offers authentic and lucid explanations of Buddhist Pali terms, with cross-references in English and source references as well. Amidst the welter of modern books on Buddhism, and translations differing one from the other, this book will help in identifying the doctrinal terms and in correcting misleading renderings. Not a mere word dictionary but an aid to the terminology of Theravada Buddhism, *Buddhist Dictionary* will be as helpful to the serious lay student as to the professional scholar.

265 pages *ISBN 955-24-0019-8*
Hardback *Price as in latest catalog*

THE BUDDHIST PUBLICATION SOCIETY

is an approved charity dedicated to making known the Teaching of the Buddha, which has a vital message for people of all creeds. Founded in 1958, the BPS has published a wide variety of books and booklets covering a great range of topics. Its publications include accurate annotated translations of the Buddha's discourses, standard reference works, as well as original contemporary expositions of Buddhist thought and practice. These works present Buddhism as it truly is—a dynamic force which has influenced receptive minds for the past two thousand years and is still as relevant today as it was when it first arose. A full list of our publications will be sent free of charge upon request. Write to:

The Hony. Secretary
BUDDHIST PUBLICATION SOCIETY
P.O. Box 61
54, Sangharaja Mawatha
Kandy   Sri Lanka